Startup 101

How to Build a Successful Business with Crowdfunding

A Guide for Entrepreneurs

Erick Walk

Copyright 2017 by Erick Walk - All rights reserved.

This document is geared towards providing exact and reliable information in regards to the topic and issue covered. The publication is sold with the idea that the publisher is not required to render accounting, officially permitted, or otherwise, qualified services. If advice is necessary, legal or professional, a practiced individual in the profession should be ordered.

- From a Declaration of Principles which was accepted and approved equally by a Committee of the American Bar Association and a Committee of Publishers and Associations.

In no way is it legal to reproduce, duplicate, or transmit any part of this document in either electronic means or in printed format. Recording of this publication is strictly prohibited and any storage of this document is not allowed unless with written permission from the publisher. All rights reserved.

The information provided herein is stated to be truthful and consistent, in that any liability, in terms of inattention or otherwise, by any usage or abuse of any policies, processes, or directions contained within is the solitary and utter responsibility of the recipient reader. Under no circumstances will any legal responsibility or blame be held against the publisher for any reparation, damages, or monetary loss due to the information herein, either directly or indirectly.

Respective authors own all copyrights not held by the publisher.

The information herein is offered for informational purposes solely, and is universal as so. The presentation of the information is without contract or any type of guarantee assurance.

The trademarks that are used are without any consent, and the publication of the trademark is without permission or backing by the trademark owner. All trademarks and brands within this book are for clarifying purposes only and are the owned by the owners themselves, not affiliated with this document.

Table of Contents

Introduction

Chapter 1: Crowdfunding – What It Is   1

    The Concept and the Highway

    Traditional Fundraising Vs Crowdfunding

    Benefits of Crowdfunding

Chapter 2: The JOBS Act   6

Chapter 3: Is Crowdfunding For You?   9

    Who and What is Crowdfunding For?

    Crowdfunding for Real Estate

    The Best Product Type for Crowdfunding

    Types of Crowdfunding

    What Makes Crowdfunding so Appealing?

Chapter 4: Step by Step Guide on How To Set Up your Crowdfunding Campaign   14

    Fundamental Crowdfunding Stages

        Step 1: Lay your groundwork.

        Step 2: Create a social media campaign.

        Step 3: Select the most suitable crowdfunding platform.

Step 4: Increase your social media footprints.

Step 5: Set your funding goal.

Step 6: Set reward tiers.

Step 7: Tell your story.

Step 8: Start your crowdfunding campaign.

Step 9: Update your donors about your progress.

Step 10: Work on your project.

Step 11: Ship your rewards.

Chapter 5: Laying The Groundwork For Your Crowdfunding Campaign   19

When is the perfect time to launch a crowdfunding campaign?

Create a Pre-campaign Project

The Pre-Crowfunding Campaign Checklist

Chapter 6: Make Your Social Media Footprints   28

Chapter 7: Select the Most Suitable Crowdfunding Platform   32

Chapter 8: Set Your Funding Goal   44

Chapter 9: Setting Reward Tiers for Your Backers   47

Chapter 10: It is Now Time to Tell Your Tale
          51

    Creating Your Pitch Text

    Creating Your Pitch Video

    Standout

Chapter 11: Start Your Crowdsourcing Campaign   57

    Secure the First 30% of Your Minimum Funding Goal

    Prepare, Launch, and Build Your Outreach

    Monitor Your Campaign Progress

Chapter 12: What To Do After The Crowdfunding Campaign Is Over   60

Chapter 13: Running An Equity Fundraising Campaign   66

Chapter 14: Crowdfunding Mistakes That You Should Avoid   72

Chapter 15: Crowdfunding Success Stories 76

Conclusion   81

Introduction

Welcome to "Startup 101 - How to Build a Successful Business with Crowdfunding."

In these pages, the author shares his insights and experience with crowdfunding. The information contained here is designed to help startup entrepreneurs and others interested or involved with it.

The second biggest reason why small and medium scale enterprises eventually fail is lack of capital – the number one reason is getting the wrong team on board. Some people might think low sales accounts as the biggest killer for small business ventures, but that is way below down there in the rankings.

Imagine that – a really significant side of the economy isn't getting funding. This is quite unfortunate since SMEs actually contribute a lot to the country's economic growth. For instance, these businesses provide 64% of all the new jobs generated each year in the United States. The overwhelming majority of companies in the US have less than 500 employees.

And this is where crowdfunding comes into the scene. It allows small and medium scale enterprises to contact and interact with investors. Eventually, the entrepreneurs who run small or medium scale businesses can tap that funding to get their company started. Their business now has a better chance to grow and make it in their respective industries. Eventually, more jobs will be created and the economy will become livelier, even healthier in fact.

The JOBS Act, particularly titles II and III have made it much easier for investors to find small businesses that require funding. The said act created exemptions to the 1933 Securities Act under 506 0 (c) and 4 (a) (6). These laws also provide protection to investors as well as afford them risk appropriate returns.

This is why a lot of talk has been generated in the recent years about the potentials of crowdfunding. However, there are several details that require one's attention when you try to take advantage of the opportunities in crowdfunding. That is the objective of this short book – to provide some guidance and insight to entrepreneurs regarding the rules, best practices, as well as the regulations involved in crowdfunding.

Crowdfunding is going to make waves in securities markets everywhere. Some people may think little of it, but it will eventually create a huge impact – they just don't know it yet. It is your privilege to take part in it now while things are just beginning to roll.

In this book, you'll learn:

- ✓ What crowdfunding is and how can you use it to fund your business
- ✓ Benefits of crowdfunding
- ✓ Different crowdfunding platforms
- ✓ Crowdfunding tips
- ✓ How to create an effective crowdfunding profile
- ✓ How to reward donors

It is my hope that the information contained in this book will help you understand how to make the most of this one of a kind opportunity. Remember that it will not be easy and it will require just as much work when you're trying to acquire funding the traditional way.

To your success!

Chapter 1

Crowdfunding – What It Is

The concept of crowdfunding isn't actually a 21st century invention. It has been around for quite a while now and people have done it, albeit successfully on many occasions. We may have given the idea a new name but the principle has been practiced and it has been proven time and again to work quite well.

Here's one example. Everyone knows the icon that is the Statue of Liberty, right? It is one of the most popular American icons. What a lot of people in the world do not realize is that it took a bit of crowdfunding to make that statue stand where it is today. How did that happen? Well, here's the story behind it.

We all know that the Lady Liberty was a gift to the Americans from the French. Simply put, the French constructed it and even paid for the transportation costs to bring it to the US. The only problem left was to get it erected on a pedestal or base – yes, the one that it's currently on, and that cost a lot of money.

In fact, the American Committee, the one that was charged with the duty of raising the needed funds, had to find a way to raise $300,000 just to construct that base. The statue was on its way to American shores and that means they were out of time. So how do you raise that kind of money?

The answer is to go to the public. Here comes Mr. Pulitzer who owns a newspaper. He published a plea the following day asking for donations. In just five months the donation campaign was able to generate $100,000. The rest of the story of course is history. And that is a fine sample of 19th century crowdfunding.

The Concept and the Highway

As you can see, the idea of going to the public to get the necessary cash to fund an enterprise isn't as new as some would assume. What made the idea difficult if not impossible is the inability to reach out to the general public. Back in the day, not everyone had a Mr. Pulitzer.

During the 1980s or the 1990s, people will have to reach out to their friends to ask for funding. This is called "solicitation" where startup entrepreneurs hand out envelopes to their friends and ask for contributions. Some startup entrepreneurs also held fund-raising parties to raise funds for their business.

Today we have one in the form of the internet – nowadays, anyone can reach out to millions. The internet has made it easier for startup entrepreneurs to raise money through the help of strangers who share the same vision.

Traditional Fundraising vs. Crowdfunding

There are a number of traditional fundraising methods that's been used by many businesses and organizations for decades, which includes direct mail, events, and door to door solicitation. Most businesses get funding by securing a bank loan or by acquiring a deal from an angel investor.

Getting a bank loan is one of the easiest fundraising methods available. But, a lot goes into it and you need to have a good credit rating to secure a bank loan. Also, first time business owners are less likely to be eligible for a bank loan, and if they do, the interest rates tend to be quite high as well.

Holding fundraising events is also a good way to secure funds for your business. But, you'd need to shell out a significant amount of money to host an event.

Crowdfunding is inexpensive and it is less time consuming. The main downside of traditional fundraising methods is that it's time consuming. You need to approach a lot of people and explain your cause. Most of the time, it would be difficult to find people who will spare a few minutes to listen to your pitch.

Benefits of Crowdfunding

Crowdfunding has a lot of benefits, which includes the following:

1. Crowfunding is a cheaper way to raise funds for your business. You do not need to shell out a lot of money to start an online crowdfunding campaign.

2. It is more efficient than traditional fundraising methods. You don't have to go "door to door" to find potential donors. You can reach millions of people in just a few clicks.

3. It builds traction. Crowdfunding is a great way to secure social proof. If a lot of people contribute and buy into your idea, others will easily follow suit. The number of pre-orders, backers, and media attention that you get from social media campaign eventually builds a lot of traction. It also helps increase the popularity and credibility of your business.

4. It enables you to fully express your vision and idea to people who will willingly listen. You are certain that the people who'll discover your page through the website are all potential investors, no bit of effort put into your campaign goes to waste because of this.

5. Crowdfunding is also a great tool for receiving feedback from other people. Suggestions on how you can further improve your product or idea are all valuable. Think of these people as

your future clients, and as such their thought counts as well.

People will willingly invest in something they believe in. Becoming part of someone's start-up right from the very seed of it is appealing both young and old investors alike. This is one of the main benefits that come with using CROWDFUNDING.

Chapter 2

The JOBS Act

The JOBS Act has created a wave of excitement over the prospects of crowdfunding. It began as the Entrepreneurs' Access to Capital Act in late 2011 while in the hands of the House of Representatives and later became the Jumpstart Our Business Startups Act in 2012 under the US Senate. The president signed it into law on April 5, 2012.

It was a badly needed piece of legislature, needless to say. With an economy in crisis, a lot of things had to change in order to stimulate economic growth and create more jobs. The Securities Act of 1933 and other laws enacted thereafter (e.g. Dodd-Frank Act and Sarbanes-Oxley Act) made it difficult, while some would say impossible, for small and medium scale businesses to access much needed funding.

This act amends provisions, laws, and regulations that have long oppressed (well, about 80 years give or take a few) and practically crushed capital formation in both the private as well as the public markets. 28 million businesses in US were practically starved of capital sources and to think they account for 64% of the net jobs produced each year.

Someone once correctly observed that the reason why America has fewer jobs is the fact that there are fewer job makers. And why are there only a few job makers? It is because securities laws have made it more difficult for smaller enterprises to access capital. President Barack Obama pointed out that "crowdfunding is the democratization of capital."

The Amendments

Title I of the JOBS Act reopened the capital markets to startup companies, making things easier for them to go public. According to the Act, any business that has revenue that is less than one billion per annum is defined as "an emerging growth company."

Title II of the Act amends Securities Act '33 Rule 506 Regulation D, which lifts the previous ban set in the rules for general solicitation. That means businesses that are on the rise can now access capital that is provided by accredited investors. Simply put, this part of the new law includes guidelines for crowdfunding for the rich.

Title III of the Act on the other hand contains amendments for Section 4, which creates exemptions so that companies can now raise capital from accredited and non-accredited investors up to 1 million dollars ($1 million or less). The mode of raising such capital is via the internet. Simply put, this is the crowdfunding for the rest of us who are not multi- millionaires. Note that both Title II and Title III of the JOBS Act create exemptions for provisions on registration as found in the Securities Act of 1933.

With the exemptions created, a lot of interest has been generated in crowdfunding. It is set to change the landscape for investors and to boost growth among small and medium enterprises.

For the full text of the amendments and exemptions made, please check www.sec.gov/spotlight/jobs-act.

Chapter 3

Is Crowdfunding For You?

Simply put, crowdfunding is a venture to raise capital via monetary contributions from a large number of people or the crowd. It is currently being used by entrepreneurs to fund various applications such as indie films, journalism, music, blogging, and especially startup companies. Civic projects have been quite successful as well as funding for a cause. It has been found that local folks tend to support local projects.

So, simply put, crowdfunding is now being used for pretty much any enterprise. Non-profit organizations have had a lot of success raising for different causes from funds to help cancer patients to school teachers requesting materials for classrooms in distress. There are also crowdfunding websites that are designed to help students and a school's faculty to receive funds for tuition needs and other projects. The funding for university crowdfunding primarily comes from the school's alumni as well as the general public pitching in.

Crowdfunding has such a dynamic capital formation infrastructure that it can also fund large scale enterprises such as real estate projects. The applications for this industry are far reaching. With it investors can pool their capital to fund mortgages, for down payments of home buyers, and the acquisition of distressed mortgages among others. Real estate crowdfunding has already seen success in many parts of the world like Europe, France, and the Middle East and it is still growing.

As mentioned earlier, you can use the crowdfunding platforms to fund just about any project. But, most companies are not a good fit for crowdfunding. Companies who have the highest success rates on these websites would be the ones who produce consumer products that are unique and of some value to its target market. The same goes for companies who have some degree of hype about them—perhaps even a fan base of dedicated consumers—tend to achieve their goals faster when it comes to crowdfunding as well.

However, this does not mean that smaller and less popular businesses can't achieve the same success. It all boils down to how you handle project and the product or service that you're offering. If it's interesting and new, people are likely to be more interested in it.

Different Types of Crowdfunding

There are different types of crowdfunding that you should be aware of. They differ in the form of contribution, return, and of course the motivation of the founder. Here are the basic four:

•*Donation Crowdfunding*: The founder of this enterprise started the campaign in order to fund charity purposes. There are social motivations behind the effort. Of course, when funds are donated you don't exactly gain any tangible benefits. It's all for a good cause anyway. A good example of this is the crowdfunding efforts done for the victims of natural calamities such as Typhoon Katrina and others. The funds for this type of crowdfunding come in the form of donations.

•*Equity Crowdfunding:* You can say that this is the opposite of donation crowdfunding where the primary motivation is financial, although some form of social and intrinsic motives does exist in these enterprises. This is the type of crowdfunding that will usually be used by startup companies and growing small businesses. Contributions in this type come in the form of investments with returns.

•*Crowdfunded Lending:* The contributions that come into this type of crowdfunding come in the form of loans. And the funds collected using this medium will be used for the repayment of loans. Of course, the funds will be paid for in a specified time with interest. Some of these endeavors are used for social and civic purposes and at sometimes the investors themselves waive the interest to help the financially distressed.

•*Reward Crowdfunding:* Investors and/or donors in this type of crowdfunding receive tangible items or

services as rewards. Some forms of contributions come in the form of a pre-purchase of the product or service being created, which will be introduced in the future.

Of the different types of crowdfunding mentioned above, investors can use reward crowdfunding and equity crowdfunding, which are more appropriate for their purposes.

What Makes Crowdfunding so Appealing?

There are several factors that have contributed to the success and appeal of crowdfunding. For one thing, it requires only a minimal amount of investment in the part of the investor who contributes to the fund. For instance, a commercial income property can be bought for only $1,000. Even those who are a bit strapped for cash can invest some money expecting a return.

Another key to its success is being able to bank on the expertise of others. You can check the profile of the executive team and judge for yourself if your investment is worth it. This also means that you have the advantage of skipping a huge chunk of the learning curve and start earning passive income by simply contributing to the capital being raised.

Another appealing factor is the fact that there is complete transparency on the part of the crowdfunding portals. Everyone who is participating can check the status of their investment as well as the status of the campaign itself. Information can be provided in real time – everything is accessed via the web.

Since everything is on the web, investors can choose any project or funding they want wherever it is available. They can even choose to invest in any property and even choose its asset class.

Downsides That You Should Know About

There are several disadvantages in crowdfunding created by the nature of the enterprise itself. For instance, investors do not have any say on how the investment will be handled. They don't get to vote, as it were, on certain investment decisions. On top of that, profits may get diluted in case additional funds are needed and more crowdfunding is done. And just like any other investment, crowdfunding also carries with it an element of risk. Note that there is no secondary market where you can sell the security that you have invested in.

Should I Try Crowdfunding?

Here's something that everyone should think about – yes, crowdfunding is a big success. However, it is still a venture. Simply put, it's not a magic pill that will kick start your business and its eventual success.

It is not always guaranteed to work. In fact, there are platforms that go on an all or nothing basis. This means that you will specify a targeted amount of capital to be raised. If the funds that have been pledged and contributed do not reach the target amount then no funding will be made and the funds will be returned to the crowd of investors.

Due diligence is required on the part of investors as well as the founders of the company – they can only exert their best effort to gain the confidence of investors and leave everything in the cloud.

Chapter 4

Step by Step Guide on How To Set Up your Crowdfunding Campaign

In this chapter you'll learn the fundamental stages of an online crowdfunding campaign, and how you can get started with your own through the use of basic steps.

Three Fundamental Stages

There are three fundamental stages of any crowdfunding campaign. First off, there is the preparation stage. The business owner gets together with his consultants, partners, lawyers, accountants, and all the necessary folks to pitch an investment idea. They prepare the marketing plan as well as the offering memorandum. Once they have that formulated, they will then post their deal online through a crowdfunding portal.

The next stage is where they raise the money. The investors post funding updates, social media posts, status updates, and also answer investor questions online. Brokers will also reach out to potential backers and media. Everyone also conducts due diligence in the process.

The crowd, on the other hand, will vet on the deal and make investments. As the investments come in, the funds are then forwarded to a bank escrow, which is FDIC insured. Notices are then sent to investors, media, and others who are concerned. If the target capital is raised or exceeded, which happens quite a number of times; then the crowdfunding portal informs the escrow of the successful closing, and then enters the third stage.

The portal then sends out commissions and blotters to brokers. The escrow then sends the funds to the founding company. The company then maintains its relationship with the investors, which means providing returns on their investment as scheduled. The company then proceeds to operate, which includes hiring employees, finding business partners, gaining customers, and making profit.

To put it simply, here are the fundamental steps that you should take in launching and managing a crowdfunding campaign:

Step 1: Set-Up the Groundwork for Your Project

Work has to start months before you launch your crowdfunding campaign. First, you have to develop the idea. Then, you have to create a prototype of the product. You have to see to it that your product is working before you even start the fund-raising campaign. If you raise funds for ideas that are impossible to execute, donors would be extremely upset and may end up accusing you of running a scam.

You also need to create a website, an approximate budget, and a robust marketing plan. Do not forget to prepare your taxes and other legal paperwork. These are all essentials to getting started with a proper business, and operating a crowdfunding project is no different. Diligence is key.

Step 2: Start Working on Your Social Media Campaign / Other Forms of Marketing
Sure, there are people who regularly look through crowdfunding websites to find interesting new projects. However, you'll gain more attention, and increase your number of investors by using social media to your advantage. Think of this as being no different from marketing your business, products and/or services. It requires most of the same strategies and the purpose is similar: Get the word out about your current campaign and entice people to participate by investing.

Step 3: Choose the Best Crowdfunding Website
There are a number of differentcrowdfunding platforms today. So, you have to choose the one that works well for you. If you're raising funds for social causes, you should try RocketHub, Crowdrise, and Causes. If you're doing a business involving creative projects, it's best to use Pubslush, Indiegogo, and Kickstarter. If you're looking for big ticket investors for your business, you can choose crowdfunding sites such as Fundable, AngelList, and Somolend.

Step 4: Set A Funding Goal
This is the trickiest part of your campaign. Some crowdfunding platforms like Kickstarter do not allow

you to keep the raised money if you have not reached the funding goal. So, it's important to set realistic funding goals. A number of projects have managed to raise more than one million dollars in investments. However, most projects, especially newer names in the business, can manage to raise at least ten thousand dollars—sometimes less.

Step 6: Set Reward Tiers
What's in it for the donors? Of course there needs to be perks for people investing in your business. More often than not, this is a tangible piece of the project such as first dibs on any prototypes that come out. You can also even offer them a small share in the business--- it all depends upon how much money they give, and what you can offer as a start-up entrepreneur. Just don't promise anything that you cannot afford to give.

Step 7: Prepare Your Pitch
For this, you need to tell people all about your project, your business, and who you are. You must properly express why you require the funding, and what you hope to achieve with the project you've put up. Text is good, but adding visuals to your page is better. Visuals will help you grab people's attention, and allow them a peek into what you're working on. Do your best to show your passion about the project and let them know about the rewards that they will get for helping out as well.

Step 8: Post Your Campaign Online
Remember to only use one website for your campaign. This would be much easier for you to look after and people will not find it suspect that you're trying to

raise funds in two different places. Just choose one platform that you trust and supports the kind of project you're working on then put all your focus into getting the word out about it. Generate interest through your campaigns, and do the hardwork needed to get people to invest in you. It won't be easy, but it is doable!

Step 9: Always Post Updates On your Page
Not only will doing so raise your credibility, it could also help increase the amount of interest directed to your project. If potential investors can see that you're doing well and putting in effort into realizing what you plan to achieve, this could motivate them into participating as well. This is particularly important for your current investors as well. Of course, they would want to see your progress and if they made the right move with helping you out. Again, photos and videos are great for this.

Step 10: Research and Improve Your Project
During the entire time you have your crowdfunding campaign up, people will likely leave you comments and suggestions on how you might improve on your product. Read through all the opinion that you receive and make sure that you consider them—both the good and the bad. The thing is, these people are your future consumers, so finding a balance between your idea and what the market demands would increase your product's profitability. People will appreciate having a voice in a business that they have put money into so do make sure you reply to their messages as well. Communication is beneficial.

Chapter 5

Establishing Your Crowdfunding Campaign

Let's look into the details of the three stages already mentioned above. There are a lot of things to remember and there are times when you may have overlooked something in the process. This is where crowdfunding consultants come in to the rescue. They can help you set things up and walk you through the entire process.

Before you even start the crowdfunding process, you must first clearly define what the project is. Since you have to convince and motivate people to give you their hard-earned money, it is important to provide them with a proper outline of what it is you want to achieve. Be honest with your purpose, of course, and do not exaggerate anything.

If you're offering a product, it would be best if you already have a sample or prototype which you can show potential investors. This provides them with a better idea of what you intend on making, how useful it would be to them, and if it it's worth the money they're putting into the project.

Most of the projects that get funded really quickly are those that offer something new or something beneficial to the consumers. So if you're only after profits, it is likely that your idea won't sell. A good idea can only take you so far—if you don't have what it takes to back it up, then it would all be for nought.

That said, what are some of the key things you should have outlined before a starting a crowdfunding campaign? Here's what you need to keep in mind:

- ✓ Cleary define your project idea – its scope, purpose, and timeline.
- ✓ Assess the feasibility and viability of your idea. You have to create something that's useful to people. If you can bring something new to the table, then all the better.
- ✓ Take time to research your targeted market. Study similar projects and how they can be improved further.
- ✓ Consider any standards and regulations that might affect your project. For example, if you're trying to produce skin care products, it's best to check several laws pertaining to cosmetics in the United States, such as the FPLA or Fair Packaging and Labeling Act and the FD&C or the Federal Food, Drug, and Cosmetic Act.
- ✓ Produce samples of your products. Yes, you will need to invest in properly presenting your product. It has to be professional and almost as good as the final item.
- ✓ Test your samples to see if your products really work. This is important once you have prototypes on hand. If there's something off about the product or it doesn't work as advertised, revise and work on it again.

- ✓ Be clear about how you want to use the crowdfunded money. Are you going to use it to produce the actual product? Are you going to use it for expansion? Are you going to use it to buy an equipment for production?

Why is this important? Well, it ensures investors that you have a clear idea when it comes to what you want to achieve. It isn't uncommon for projects to fail even whilst gaining a lot of investors. In fact, there has been plenty of cases where entrepreneurs weren't able to deliver on what they promised, and this can leave their credibility and business completely tainted. Just take this company for example:

In 2015, Torquing Group Limited has launched a crowdfunding campaign to raise funds for a small drone called Zano. But, after the company raised more than two million dollars of capital, the project was killed off because Zano was not as good as the creators have hoped it would be. The product sucked.

Twelve thousand two hundred people donated to the project and around three thousand people pre-ordered the product. But, out of that number, only 600 people got a functioning product. Torquing also promised features that they could not deliver – panorama, thermal imaging cameras, high definition video recording, and built-in audio recording.

The company spent all the money they raised hiring firmware engineers, software engineers, web developers, and marketers. Although there was no evidence that Torquing tried to scam the donors, the twelve thousand people who contributed money for the project are extremely upset.

THIS is why you have to be clear as to what your product is about. Avoid promising features that you cannot deliver. If you promise something that you cannot deliver, you'll lose credibility as an entrepreneur.

When is the perfect time to launch a crowdfunding campaign?

A crowdfunding campaign usually runs for about thirty to ninety days. So, it's best to create a crowdfunding campaign about six months (or earlier) before your target product launch date. If your product is a seasonal item, meaning it's most effective during a particular time of the year, then launch your campaign a good six months ahead of that. This provides you with enough time allowance to release the product and get it to the market before the season comes.

You can look at the pre-campaign as a way to test the waters even before you launch your actual crowdfunding campaign. There are services and sites that allow you to create a page that announces your intent to create a crowdfunding campaign.

The Pre-Crowfunding Campaign Checklist

Here's a list of the things that you should do before you start your pre-crowdfunding campaign.

- ✓ **Put up a website or a landing page.**

The idea is to make the announcement to let people know about the idea. If you're producing an organic acne control product, for example, you can post the photos of your product samples on your website. You can also include the product information – ingredients, benefits, how it's made, etc.

Use your business website to tell your story and market your product. Make sure that it loads quickly and that it looks good on mobile devices. Also, include a "call to action" content that encourages your website visitors to support your upcoming crowdfunding campaign. It's also best to include "behind the scenes" pictures. This way, potential donors get to know your work a little bit more.

- ✓ **Build an all star campaign team.**

A crowdfunding campaign that's run by a team earns more than three times as much as the crowdfunding campaigns that are created by individuals. This is because working with a team widens your network, increasing the reach of your campaign. Having a team also allows you to focus more on the tasks that you're skilled at. Your crowdfunding team members don't have to be your employees. They can be your colleagues, family members, friends, or people you trust.

Aside from the team who will help you manage your crowdfunding page. You may also have to reach out to people who can help you with product shots, graphic design, and pitch videos. Of course, you can do these things by yourself. But, outsourcing the services of a professional photographer or graphic artist can save you a lot of time and it helps ease your workload. It also guarantees that you'll end up with high-quality and professional-looking output.

✓ **Create a mailing list.**

After preparing your pitch text, pitch videos, project plan, and budget, you will then have to collect emails and build your mailing list. The list of emails you collect will be from prospects and other interested parties who pledge to inform others about your crowdfunding campaign through social media and other methods when you launch it.

You can use these tips in creating a mailing list:

- Collect business cards – When you attend networking events, ask for people's business cards. This will help you build your mailing list.

- Use a sign up sheet – When you are showcasing your product at a trade show, ask the booth visitors to place their names and email address on a sign up sheet.
- Ask website visitors to enter their email address – You can give away a free ebook in exchange of an email.

Note that you are not yet soliciting investments, what you are looking for are people who are willing to share your investment idea to the crowd. The typical pre-campaign period lasts from 60 up to 90 days. That's how much time you have to craft the pitch for your campaign. The more emails you have in your mailing list the bigger the chances of success.

Accounting, Taxes, and All the Legal Stuff

While you're polishing things up you should take care of all the taxes and legal matters before you start your actual crowdfunding project. If you still don't have a business bank account, then get one. This is where your CPA will become a big help to you. You also need help to set up an LLC or a limited liability company. Forming a business before you even start your crowdfunding campaign increases your credibility.

Here are a few steps that you should take in turning your project into a legitimate business:

1. Choose the name of your LLC.

2. File the "articles of organization". The requirements vary from state to state.
3. Pay the filing fees. The fees usually amount to around $100. You must also pay the annual tax on top of the filing fees.
4. Create the LLC operating agreement.
5. Publish a notice in a local newspaper. Some states require this.
6. Get permits and licenses.

You must also seek legal services in dealing with the following issues:

- ✓ **Tax.** The revenue that you derive from pre-sale and rewards may be subject to taxes. You can either consult a tax lawyer or an experienced accountant to help you out with taxes and exemptions, if there's any.
- ✓ **Intellectual Property.** Many entrepreneurs were sued because they used someone else's copyrighted photos or videos without permission. For example, Ultra sued Michelle Phan for using Kaskade's music without permission. Also, note that there are many corrupt entrepreneurs who steal ideas from crowdfunding projects on Kickstarter and Indiegogo.

Before you start the campaign, you should make an outline of all your project-related expenses and account for all the contributions. You can do this yourself if we're only talking about a few thousand dollars. But, if you're planning on raising more than ten thousand dollars. It's a good idea to ask for help from an accountant.

Chapter 6

Establish Your Business through Social Media

Social media is one of the biggest free tools in your hands, so take advantage of it. You need to create and bolster your social media presence. It doesn't matter how few/many people you have following you on Twitter or your Facebook page, you will eventually need more if you want your crowdfunding venture to succeed.

There are social media tools and services that you can subscribe to in order to boost your social media presence and gauge your current reach. Note that you will need around 1,000 to 3,000 new followers per month to ensure the success of your pre-campaign.

Note that building an audience in social media will take a good deal of time. Best practice is to allot at least 3 to 6 months before actually launching your crowdfunding campaign. If your funding goals are larger and your type of crowdfunding a bit more complex (e.g. you need higher tier investors) then you will need more time to build your social media reach – you can also measure that by your current follower count. It's also a good idea to use the social media site that you're most comfortable with.

One of the best ways to increase your social media reach is to ask help from someone who has influence over a number of people. They need not be a celebrity, but a person who has a bigger voice in the target market you're after would be very effective for this purpose. Yes, there is some investment needed for this unless you can manage a decente exchange deal with your social media influencer.

But what if you don't have the money to fund that? Don't fret. You can make do without the help of a social media influencer—but you need to put in a lot of work.

Here are some tips to help boost your social media presence:

1. Create teasers and post them in your social media accounts.
2. Find hashtags which are related to your campaign. Hashtags increases the reach of your post and it also increases engagement. Just make sure you keep from spamming said hashtags as these might bother other users.
3. Check Facebook insights to see the performance of your posts based on comments, shares, demographics, reach, and like.
4. Use social networking sites as testing laboratories. Use Facebook or Twitter to check market response and viability.
5. Engage with your audience and respond to comments. Be as friendly as you can when replying to messages and queries. Also, encourage your social media followers to give you feedback. This will help you improve your campaign and product.

6. If you're able to, hiring a social media manager is great for this purpose. They would be able to devote all their time and energy into increasing your brand's relevance and be able to do research on your behalf.
7. Display your "behind the scenes" photos on your social media account. This way, potential donors can see how you and your team worked hard to transform your idea into reality.
8. Make your audience feel that their financial contributions to your project and business can and will make a difference.
9. Remember that you cannot please everybody. So, you have to focus on a specific group of people that's interested in the your business. Once you determine your target market, you have to create social content that appeals to your target market. Again, for this, market research is key. Make full use of visuals, language, and aesthetics to appeal to your target market.
10. Keep your posts short and sweet. Remember that people do not have time to read long posts. So, you have to keep your posts short and direct to the point.
11. Do not focus on quantity. Focus on quality. You do not have to post on Facebook or Twitter daily. But, when you do, make sure that you post engaging content. Also, make sure that you post something that people want to share.

12. Pour your heart into your social media posts. Make sure that your posts showcase your heart and your passion.
13. Run ads and sponsored stories. If you're planning to raise tens and thousands of dollars, you cannot reply on organic reach alone. You may have to pay a few dollars to increase your post reach. Facebook ads don't cost much. You can launch a seven day Facebook advertising campaign for just $30.
14. Do not abandon your social media followers after you've raised the funds. You have to keep engaging them. You must regularly post updates on the progress of the project.

Social media is a powerful tool that you can use to create a successful crowdfunding campaign. It allows you to reach more people and establish yourself as an expert in your industry.

Chapter 7

Select the Most Suitable Crowdfunding Platform

There are a lot of crowdfunding platforms to choose from. The type of platform you choose will depend on the type of crowdfunding you want to put up. The most popular of these crowdfunding platforms are Indiegogo and Kickstarter. However, it doesn't necessarily mean that you need to sign up with those two or any of the really popular platforms.

They are not always your best bet. Now, you also have to consider the fact that you are not the only one putting up a campaign – you're actually competing with millions of other entrepreneurs and businesses who also need funds.

Do your own research and categorize your funding needs according to its niche. If you are trying to establish a mini- IPO that will require around 50 million dollars in capital, which takes advantage of Regulation A+ in the JOBS Act, then you may look for platforms that cater to these such as Bankroll Ventures.

In case you're trying to fund your next music video or music album then you can look into creative funding provided by platforms such as Tubestart, Tunefund, and the like. Now, you should also consider the size of the platform. The smaller crowdfunding platforms can offer you niche specific features that may not always be present in the bigger platforms today.

If you're looking to fund an app developer company then you may want to look into Appbackr. If your project has something to do with journalism, then check out the offerings at Emphasis. If you're looking for funding coming from local members of a certain community then you should try out Bolstr.

If you're raising funds for equity in your project then you may want to see how Fundable can help you iron things out. If your project is technology related then check out Seedinvest. If your project has been denied by one of the larger crowdfunding sites, like Kickstarter for instance, then there is a crowdfunding platform for you too – Crowdfunder.

Here's a list of the best crowdfunding platforms:

1. Kickstarter

Kickstarter is one of the most popular crowdfunding platforms. This website helps musicians, film-makers, artists, and budding entrepreneurs bring their projects to life. The website was launched in 2009 and has since helped more than one hundred thirty projects get funded. The company is based in New York and it was founded by Charles Adler, Yancey Strickler, and Perry Chen. The website was built using the funding acquired from angel investors such as Zach Klein, Caterina Fake, and Jack Dorsey.

Kickstarter has funded a lot of famous artists, animators, film-makers, and musicians such as TLC, Amanda McBroom, Amanda Palmer, Paula Cole, Jennifer Paige, Whoopi Goldberg, Zach Braff, Tom Rush, Kristen Bell, Rand Miller, Don Bluth, Gary Hustwit, Spencer Tunick, Dan Harmon, and Rand Miller.

The platform has managed to raised millions of dollars for projects like Pebble, Coolest Cooler, Exploding Kittens, and Fidget cube.

Campaign Rules

Kickstarter funding is an "all" or "nothing" game. You must set a campaign goal – the total amount of money that you need to complete your project at a given deadline. You will not get the funding unless the campaign goal is reached.

Project creators must offer rewards to their backers – there are no stringent rules on the KIND of reward you give, as long as the investors are well aware of what it is. There is a list of prohibited items available on the website so it would do you good to check that whilst you're drafting potential rewards to give investors.

Kickstarter is very creative project centric—that is: it supports various project categories such as comics, art, crafts, technology, theater, music, video, film, design, dance, music, journalism, and photography. You can't use this platform to fund a business that raises money for charities and advocacies.

2. Indiegogo

Indiegogo is a crowdfunding site that was founded in 2008 by Slava Rubin, Danae Ringelmann, and Eric Schell. Their headquarters is located in San Francisco, California. The website operates on a reward-based system. This means that investors and donors who are willing to fund a project gets a gift, not an equity stake. It has managed to raise more than one million dollars for "Let's Build A Goddamn Tesla Museum" and more than five million dollars for Code.org. So, it's no wonder that Indiegogo is popular amongst entrepreneurs.

<u>Campaign Rules</u>

You can create a campaign on Indiegogo to reach out to "donors" or "contributors". But, you must be at least eighteen years old to launch a project without parental consent. Campaign owners between the ages of thirteen and seventeen should secure their parent's consent before they can launch a campaign. You can use IndieGogo to fund various projects such as tech innovations, books, magazines, photography, podcasts, film, music, video games, tabletop games, dance, theater, comics, and film. You can also use this platform to raise funds for community projects that would help promote education, animal rights, human rights, environment, and spiritual pursuits. You can even use it to raise funds for museum or temple construction.

You are not allowed to raise funds for illegal activities or projects that infringe any copyright, trade secret, trademark, or patent.

You must also provide perks to donors in exchange for their contributions. But, you are not allowed to offer prohibited rewards such as financial incentive, profit sharing, equity, bonds, plane tickets, drugs, lottery tickets, raffle tickets, bones, skulls, alcohol, and ammunition.

3. GoFundMe

GoFundMe is a crowdfunding website which is mostly used for personal causes and not much for entrepreneurial projects. It was founded in 2010 by Brad Damphousse and Andrew Ballester. It is considered as the biggest crowdfunding platform to date.

How It Works

GoFundMe allows users to create a website showcasing their projects and causes. This platform allows the users to share their causes via social network links and email. People can donate to the cause using a debit or credit card. The company generates revenue by deducting a five percent transaction fee from each donation.

GoFundMe is not an incentive-based crowdsourcing platform. Although musicians and artists have raised money using this site, the platform was primarily designed for personal causes such as payment for medical bills. The website even has a special section for students raising money for their education.

4. Patreon

Patreon is a membership crowdsourcing platform that provides business tools for content creators such as web comic artists, YouTube videographers, musicians, artists, and writers. It was established in 2013 by a web developer named Sam Yam and a musician named Jack Conte.

How It Works

Content creators can set up a page on the Patreon website and their "patrons" can pay their chosen creators on a monthly basis. Each creator can set a maximum limit for the amount that they will receive each month. Patrons, on the other hand, can choose to cancel their payment anytime. Creators usually provide specific benefits to their patrons such as exclusive content or access to behind-the-scenes videos.

5. Pledgemusic

PledgeMusic is a fundraising platform for artists and music producers. It is also a "direct-to-fan" music platform that enables musicians to market, distribute, and pre-sell their music videos, concerns, and recordings. A lot of artists have launched a campaign through PledgeMusic, including Erasure, Slash, Kate Nash, Ash, and Sum 41. This platform boasts a 90% campaign success rate, which is much higher than Indiegogo and Kickstarter.

How It Works

Pledgemusic has three campaign options for the budding musician – the funding period campaign, the pre-order campaign, and the number of units campaign. To launch a campaign, you need to set a goal amount and a campaign period. Pledgemusic will refund all contributions if the amount was not reached. If you meet the campaign goal, Pledgemusic deducts 15%of your total contributions.

6. RocketHub

This crowdsourcing platform is used by various filmmakers, photographers, musicians, entrepreneurs, philanthropists, game developers, scientists, and fashion designers. It was launched in 2010 and the company is based in New York City.

How It Works

Users can launch a campaign in RocketHub to fund various creative and entrepreneurial projects. It allows users to set a deadline and funding goal. Users must also offer "perks" in exchange for contributions. The company deducts four percent from the total amount collected and charges four percent for processing fees. So, the company collects a total of eight percent. But, the good thing about this platform is that it allows users to keep the collected funds even if the target amount was not reached by the deadline.

7. Crowdfunder

This website offers equity funding and revenue sharing deals to venture capitalists. It's also a platform that entrepreneurs and artists can use to fund their projects. Aside from equity and revenue sharing deals, this site also allows entrepreneurs get a loan. This platform is used by entrepreneurs in various industries such as finance, technology, business to business marketing, hospitality, food, beverage, lifestyle, mobile gaming, and real estate. The site has raised millions of dollars to various projects and companies such as Style Lend, Gigwell, EyeCam, Rageon, Shipsi, and Ambygear.

8. Appbckr

Appbckr, as the name suggests, is a crowdfunding site for app developers. It is not as popular as most crowdfunding sites on this page, but it does provide a very specific for entrepreneurs who want to launch their own apps. It's worth checking out, despite being a new name in the industry.

9. Lending Club

This is a "peer to peer" lending company based in San Francisco, California. It was founded in 2007 and it was first launched as a Facebook app. This platform enables followers to acquire unsecured personal loans from one thousand dollars to forty thousand dollars.

How It Works

The borrowers can create a loan listing within the Lending Club website. They can input information about themselves and the project they want to get funded. But, a word of warning, you must have a good credit rating to secure funding. You can pay the loan anytime without penalty.

10. AngelList

AngelList is the ultimate fund-raising platform for startups. It's known as the "LinkedIn of Startups". This website was created for:

- ✓ Startups who want to get funded
- ✓ Angel investors
- ✓ Job-seekers who want to work in startups

This crowd funding platform was founded by Babak Nivi and Naval Ravikant. The platform has already funded more than two hundred forty startups and which was backed by around 2,673 investors. It allows small time entrepreneurs to have access to venture capital.

11. Ulele

Ulele is dubbed as the first European crowdfunding website. It was built to fund original and unique projects. It was founded by Thomas Grange and Alexandre Boucherot in Paris on October 2010. This crowdfunding platform allows entrepreneurs and artists to launch projects wherever they may be in the world. However, there is some restriction to this as you will need to have a SEPA or North American bank account as this company can only transfer funds to these countries.

How it Works

You just need to create your page in four easy steps. Then, you need to share the page for the world to see. This platform allows people to fund projects via debit cards, credit cards, and PayPal. This crowdfunding platform supports twenty three currencies including the U.S. Dollar, Danish Krone, Canadian Dollar, Japanese Yen, Philippine Peso, New Zealand Dollar, Australian Dollar, Swiss Franc, Taiwan Dollar, South African ZAR, Thai Baht, Polish Zloty, Czech Koruna, British Pound, Euro, Hungarian Forint, and Hong Kong dollar.

QUESTION: *Should I just start my own crowdfunding platform?*

Now that is an interesting question. Do take note that the cost of putting up a platform will vary depending on how it is targeted. That means you need to have a well-defined niche that you will serve. It will also require a lot of time and effort not only to build the website but also to run the community of people who will be involved in the portal.

The initial cost of starting a platform will be around $5,000 to $10,000 a year, just like starting a really huge website. If you're going to run a smaller site, then it will cost you around $20 each month. There are sites and services that can help you build a fully functional crowdfunding platform for about $100 per month, like www.crowdfundingapp.co and others.

However, note that that is just the initial cost. Note that creating a new fund portal will be like starting your own company; that is if you're in it for the long haul. That means you shouldn't be surprised that when you make your feasibility analysis that you will have to come up with a starting capital of $250,000 and more.

Chapter 8

Set Your Funding Goal

While some members of your staff are busy with building your mailing list, social media, legal matters, and working with the crowdfunding platform, it is now time to get your executive team's heads together to determine your funding goal. This of course will be submitted to the platform you will be selecting.

A lot of advice and opinion have been given when it comes to setting the fund amount. Well, the fact is that a lot of it is still out there and the math isn't really solid. Note that everyone's situation is absolutely unique, so you can't really give any hard and fast rules on how to actually set a funding goal.

Building a startup can incur a number of costs such as money needed for: advertising, research expenses, product development costs, employee salaries, technological expenses, supplies, and equipment. You should also incorporate legal costs, permits, insurance, and license fees. Always take the time to compute these costs, so you'd know how much you need to launch your project.

You should also incorporate some of the crowdfunding costs, such as:

•Costs for PR as well as marketing costs – You would encounter a number of marketing costs for: special events, product sample costs, travel expenses, and print material costs. If you choose to work with a public relations firm, this is also going to cost you a chunk of money. Of course, you always have the option of DIY.

•Total cost of fulfilling the rewards you will promise in your pitch – You would have to pay shipping and delivery costs. These "rewards" may be taxable, too.

•Processing fees – Most crowdfunding platforms use third party payment processing systems. This is the reason why they charge processing fees.

•Fees that will be collected by the crowdfunding platform – Crowdfunding platforms keep five to fifteen percent of the total funds raised. So, you must make room for this fee in your budget.

•A cushion fund or buffer amount just in case things go awry – This can go anywhere from 20% to 40% of your computations.

CAVEAT: And now comes the hard truth – you should know about this so here it is. Only a select few crowdfunding campaigns, so far, have been able to raise funds more than $100,000. The actual effects of the exemptions created in the JOBS Act are yet to be seen, but it may boost investor confidence. That may also mean that more campaigns will be able to successfully raise more capital in the future when everything is fully implemented, perhaps even breaking the $100K barrier.

Here's another thing you should think about. If you set a fund goal that is way too high then you may be preventing smaller investors and backers from joining in. Remember that the idea is to be able to reach the funding goal at an earlier date (the sooner the better) so that you will have more time to raise extra funds to stretch your capital funding allowance. Remember that a crowdfunding campaign also has a deadline to be met.

Also, you cannot rely solely on the crowdfunding campaign to back your project. You must also think of other ways to raise the capital you need. This is because there's no guaranteeing the success of your project. You might reach you goal, you might even exceed it—but there's also a chance that it would fail and won't garner the interest you were hoping for. Always have a back-up plan if this is a project that you truly want to see established.

Chapter 9

Setting Reward Tiers for Your Backers

This is the step that allows you to cheat a little bit. You see, you are not the first one to put up a crowdfunding campaign. In fact, you can bet your bottom dollar that someone else has already put up a successful crowdfunding campaign that is a lot like the one you are concocting.

The good news is that the many different crowdfunding portals can give you historical data that you can work with – especially when setting up reward tiers for your backers. Note that Indiegogo has already indicated that the most popular price point for reward tiers on their portal is at $25.

That figure can change so it will be better to check out the data in different portals and then carefully decide yours.

Setting reward tiers will encourage donors to shell out bigger amounts for your projects. Here's a list of rewards ideas that you can use for your campaign. Remember that no matter what the dollar value of the donation is, you should offer a reward that's meaningful for backers. Here's a sample reward tier that you can follow:

$1 to $5 Donations

- ✓ Acknowledgement on your project's website
- ✓ A personal thank you card

- ✓ Placing the donor's name in the credits

$10 to $25

- ✓ Electronic version of your product
- ✓ Invitations to your project launching party
- ✓ Finished version of toys and games

$25 to $50

- ✓ One piece of your finished product
- ✓ Signed copy of your printed product

$100 and up

- ✓ Multiple copies of your products
- ✓ Printed "thank yous" on the label of your product

Here's a number of reward ideas that you can give to donors who contributed $25 and above:

1. A flash drive containing your work and the behind the scenes footage. For example, if you're producing bamboo bicycles, you can include the video showing how each bicycle is made.
2. If you're raising funds for a food business, you can send recipe books to your donors.
3. You can mail autograph script pages.
4. Custom smartphone cases
5. Printed shirts that say "I helped fund (the product name)".
6. Put the donors' name in the credits.
7. Vanity plate

8. Invitation to a dinner party
9. Customized bumper stickers
10. Customized mugs
11. If you're an artist and a donor pledged $10,000, it's a good idea to paint a mural on your donor's home or building.
12. The costumes and clothes of your actors and actresses
13. Refrigerator art
14. Free beats from your album
15. Handwritten postcards
16. Share secret tips
17. Ukelele lessons via Skype
18. Beautiful calendars
19. Food tasting party
20. Craft supplies
21. VIP meet and greet
22. A basket filled of picnic supplies
23. Spa day
24. Special edition of your product
25. If you're building a barn, you can name a horse or a goat after a donor.

Here's a list of additional reward tips that you can use in keeping your donors and investors happy:

1. Check the terms of your chosen crowdfunding platform to determine which reward items are allowed or prohibited. Some crowdfunding sites allow entrepreneurs to give out food items as rewards while some prohibit it.

2. Provide valuable rewards to backers who choose to donate huge amounts of money to your project.
3. Most people donate money because they want to feel like they're part of something bigger than them. So, share the project's story on your website and make a feature on backers who pledge $500 or more.
4. Choose quality over quantity.
5. Find a way to use rewards as promotional tools for your projects. For example, you can give away caps or mugs which have the logo of your product on them.
6. Always focus on "what's in it for them". This mindset helps you create terms and rewards that can help you raise all the amount that you're looking for.
7. One of the best ways to reward your donors is to engage them and make them feel like they are part of something. Ask your donors to also encourage their friends, family, and colleagues to contribute to your project. You can even ask donors to contribute ideas to make your project better.

Gratitude is one of the best virtues one could have. It's good for your soul and also good for your business. So, make sure to let your investors know how you appreciate their contributions to your project. Who knows? You may be needing their help again in the near future.

Chapter 10

Share Your Story and Your Passion for the Project

You will be required to tell your story – you need to describe the campaign that you are putting up and it will be seen by visitors and potential investors to your campaign page on the crowdfunding portal. You can think of it as your executive summary.

You should tell the public what your project is all about, why you need the money, and what you have to offer in return. This of course is your sales pitch and you only have 400 to 600 words to make it really convincing.

You should add photos, your prototypes (in case you're introducing a new product), song samples, interactive tools, and videos in your message. Do everything possible to drive the message home and help investors understand why they need to support your campaign. Remember to keep things clear and concise – don't beat around the bush, get to the point and try to make an impression.

Putting Your Pitch Together: The Essentials

Your crowdfunding pitch is the essay that tells people about your project, about yourself, your business, and why you choose to pursue this idea. Remember that this is the first thing people would read on your page and it could make or break your chances of gaining potential investors.

Here a few simple tips that you can use in writing your pitch text:

- ✓ **Tell your story.** Write about who you are and how you came up with the project. Are you a software engineer creating an app that makes people's lives easier? Are you a recovering shopaholic producing inexpensive clothing? Honesty is key here. Be sincere with your words.
- ✓ **What your project is for.** You must outline how your project can help or what the purpose for it is. Not all projects focus on certain advocacies; some are meant to simply create a new form of entertainment for other people. The important thing here is that you're able to share why you're so passionate about pursuing this project, and why you believe it could be of some use to other people as well. There's always room for ideas, no matter how unique.
- ✓ **Be specific.** This refers to the funding goal you've set and what you intend to use the money for. It is best to be transparent when it comes to these things. Are you using the funding to create prototypes? Perhaps to develop the final product? Or are you using it for further research before finalizing your idea? Be specific, be clear, and outline everything.

✓ **Proofread your pitch text**. Last, but not the least, always proofread your work. Check for any errors or inconsistencies. Read through it to see if you were able to express yourself properly, using the right words to say what you mean. Get a friend to help out. Two perspectives are always better than one.

Most of all, keep your pitch text short and simple. Avoid using jargon and complicated words. Do not write to impress, but write to capture the hearts of potential donors.

Creating Your Pitch Video

For some people, visuals are more effective in expressing their ideas than text. If you think about it, too, people tend to be more receptive when images are involved. Creating a video to go along with your pitch isn't that difficult, you just need to keep in mind your goal and make sure that you keep it simple. If you add one too many layers to your story, this could easily cause it to veer off of the intended purpose and confuse whoever's watching it.

Use visuals to your advantage and maximize their potential. Also, the shorter the video, the better it'll maintain people's attention. Try and fit everything into a minute long video—this length is also easily shareable on different social media websites. Save the longer ones for your own Youtube Channel, where you can go in depth with your project and what goes into it.

To help get you started, here's what you need to keep in mind:

1. Your video should answer the big question – "why should I fund your campaign?". Remember that crowdfunding is not just about asking people for money. It is about asking people to join you in a mission to make the world a better (or at least a fun) place to live in. Your video should showcase how your product can solve problems that many people encounter on a daily basis.
2. Place the important piece of information in the first fifteen seconds of your video. In this modern world, not everyone has the time to watch a two minute video. So, you have to be succinct and get to the point. Also, keep your videos short. Again, people do not have a lot of time to watch pitch videos.
3. Include charts and statistics to build trust and increase your credibility.
4. Close the video with a call to action. Ask the viewers to contribute or share the video on social networking sites.
5. Be authentic. Donors can smell pretense from afar. Take time to talk about yourself, your team, and why you believe in this project. Talk about how driven and passionate you are.
6. Be creative. There are hundreds, if not thousands, of pitch videos so you have to use your creativity to make your video stand out.

Turn your pitch video into a beautiful sixty minute movie that showcases your product.
7. Make your video funny, witty, and catchy.
8. Turn your pitch video into a marketing campaign. Create a video that appeals to both investors and potential customers. This allows you to hit two birds with one stone.
9. Put yourself in the shoes of your potential donors to understand them and to see what touches their hearts and make them reach for their checkbooks.

Watch these videos for awesome pitch video samples for ideas:

https://www.youtube.com/watch?v=H0gUTJWrd34

https://www.youtube.com/watch?v=aShKYQ4zu8M

https://www.youtube.com/watch?v=MpmIdw5JhmU

If you wish to include the video, then remember that it doesn't have to sound like a National Geographic special presentation or something that get nods in Hollywood. Potential investors already know that you need funds and so the video quality can be excused. Best practice shows that videos that are sincere, genuine, and engaging have a tendency to capture the crowd better even if it's only three or four minutes long.

How to Make Your Campaign Standout

There are hundreds of entrepreneurs asking for funding. So, you must standout. Don't be afraid to show your humor, passion, and quirkiness. You must also show your competence. Humility is not a virtue that you must embrace when delivering a pitch. You must embrace and brag about your achievements. This is the only way that you could get people to invest in your project. Because, when someone donates money on your business venture, they are actually betting their money on you.

TIP: Don't ask for money at the onset. That usually turns people off. Besides, they already know that you're there to ask for funds. Instead, tell your story, and do it with enthusiasm and confidence that the project will become really successful. Remember that the crowd is trying to decide if their investment in your idea will give them the profits and other gains that you are promising.

You should also try to build more interest in the close of your pitch. If you already have a small community of believers then you can include that in your pitch as well.

Chapter 11

Start Your Crowdsourcing Campaign

Secure the First 30% of Your Minimum Funding Goal

Now this is the hardest part of the entire process. Early on you have set your funding goal. This time you should establish your minimum capital needs and then contact family, friends, business partners, and anyone you're really close to in order to make sure that you can reach up to 30% of your minimum funding goal.

Why do you need to do this? Well, think about it, compare the chances of people who know and trust you to provide funds for a venture to a total stranger who has no clue as to who you are and what you're actually capable of. If you really want that ship to sail, so to speak, those to whom you have established a relationship of trust should be willing to pitch in and make their pledges.

On top of that they should also contribute to your social media campaign in order to make your endeavor viral. That gives you a more attractive environment to convince a complete stranger to invest in your project. Pledges alone are hard to come by, actual investments are actually a bit down the funnel.

It's never easy, but with enough hard work and effort, it can be done.

Prepare, Launch, and Build Your Outreach

Your PR campaign as well as your media outreach will play a huge role in your success. Bloggers and journalists also play a key role in getting the word out. Now, with regard to media outlets, remember that time is an essential factor for these folks. Don't expect support from them if your campaign can no longer be considered newsworthy. Simply put, you scratch their back and they scratch yours.

Make it a point to partner with bloggers and media that have successfully covered campaigns that are also in your niche. There are tools that you can use to identify influencers, bloggers, journalists, and other content publishing sites that can help you expand your reach.

As you launch your crowdfunding campaign you will need to answer investor inquiries in social media, emails, and in the crowdfunding portal page that you have put up. Brokers will be there to provide support by reaching out to partners and other potential people and businesses that will back your campaign.

Monitor Your Campaign Progress

You must take time to monitor the progress of your campaign daily. Any day you slack off might actually cost you potential investors so be consistent with the work and effort you put into things. Monitor your progress and you'll also learn more about the market you're going after. Use what you learn to further improve the marketing you do for the campaign.

Chapter 12

What To Do After The Crowdfunding Campaign Is Over

So, you have raised the needed funds to get your project started, now what? Well, what it means is that you have successfully completed the first part of your project. The real work begins now. After all, getting funded is just the first step towards your actual goal, and that is producing results.

But before that, here are some of the things you need to remember.

Fulfilling Rewards and Providing Results

Crowdfunding platforms has helped plenty of artists and entrepreneurs bring their project to life. But, these platforms has also attracted a number of scammers, too. A quick online search would provide you with information on "Scampaigns" which are basically campaigns that produced no fruit, and where the person behind it simply ran away with the money they've raised. Sometimes, even the smallest bit of misunderstanding can cause your reputation to crumble and for all your plans to fall apart. Prevent that by keeping these things in mind:

- ✓ Be honest. As you know, dishonesty is a sure way to kill your credibility. Be upfront with your investors and be as transparent as possible when it comes to what the money is being used for.

- ✓ Ship your rewards in a timely manner to keep your donors happy. If you've provided them with a date, make sure that you follow through with it. Should it happen that you're unable to, always provide them with updates and keep them reassured that you're working on getting the rewards to them.

- ✓ Do not exaggerate the features and use of your product. Do not make promises that you can't deliver. For example, iBackPack managed to raise $750,000 on IndieGogo in 2015. The company promised to produce an urban backpack that could charge, store, and provide hotspots for iPhones. Groundbreaking, right? But, after raising $750,000, iBackPack just disappeared. The videos were taken down as if it did not exist. The company claimed that the backpack had some problems, but this did not fully explain what happened to the money. The same goes for Elio motors. They launched a crowdfunding campaign in 2014 for a gas efficient three-wheeled vehicle. The campaign raised about $17 million, but by the end of September in 2016, Elio motors was already bankrupt. Much of the money went to various "soft expenses" or paychecks. A lot of people suspected that the crowdfunding campaign was, in fact, a scam.

- ✓ Do not forget about your donors and investors. Make sure that you report progress to them. This way, they'll know that their money did not go to waste. Update them regularly so they'll feel like they are part of the project.

Most people expect to go right into development and production right after achieving their funding goals. However, things don't always go that smoothly or quickly. There is a process involved still and there would be unexpected hiccups along the way. These are all normal occurences, of course. So, with that in mind, here's what you can do to keep things moving whilst you wait for the funds to come through.

- ✓ You won't receive the funds right away. It may take weeks before you see the funds on your bank account. A lot of factors can slow down the disbursement process such as missing bank information, mistyped information, and intermediary banks. So, don't commit to pay suppliers right after your crowdfunding campaign is over.

- ✓ You do not have to waste time emailing all your donors one by one. Use "mail merge" in Outlook to email your donors. This email feature allows you to group your funders by reward level and then, create custom emails for each reward group. You can get a downloadable fulfillment information from your Kickstarter or Indiegogo dashboard. Here's a link that will help you set up mail merge in Outlook https://lifehacker.com/5508283/how-to-set-up-a-mail-merge-in-gmail-for-personalized-mass-emails.

- ✓ Sometimes, shit just happens. Your printer dies. Your artist moves to another country. Your supplier can't give you the rate you hoped for. This may mean that you have to push your reward delivery date by a few months. When these things happen, be honest to your funders. Tell them why you can't deliver the rewards right away.

- ✓ Find other ways to fund your project. You can't rely on crowdfunding alone. To scale up your business, you have to do your best to increase your sales to generate more revenue and profit.

- ✓ Lastly, it's okay to launch another campaign in the case the funds you raised was not enough.

What To Do If Your CrowdFunding Campaign Fails

Crowdfunding is a great way to get your business funded. But, it's not as easy as it looks. Not all crowdfunding projects succeed. In fact, crowdfunding has an average success rate of about fifty percent. This means that half of the crowdfunding campaigns don't reach their goals.

However, this isn't the end of the road for you. You can always start again, wiser and better informed this time. Here are the things that you can do should your campaign fail.

1. Review your campaign and try to figure out what went wrong. Is it your product? Was there a problem with your marketing campaign? Did you fail to prepare for the campaign? You see, the number one reason why a crowdfunding campaign fails is failure to do the groundwork. You have to make sure that everything is in place before you even start launching your crowdfunding campaign.

2. Treat crowdfunding as more than just a way to raise funds. You must also see it as product validation. If only a few people donated to your campaign, maybe your product is not interesting, useful, or good enough. So, you have to find ways to improve your product.

3. Also, you need to examine your crowdfunding campaign. Is crowdfunding really for you? Is it fit for the kind of product that you're producing? If not, then it's good to try other types of fund-raising.

Chapter 13

Running An Equity Fundraising Campaign

You can raise money for your business on Kickstarter or Indiegogo in exchange for rewards. But, if you're planning to aim for high ticket investors and you're planning to give away equity as rewards, that's a whole different story.

First, you should ask if you are ready for an equity crowdfunding campaign? Are you confident that you can reach the campaign goal within the deadline? Do you have all the necessary paperwork?

Here are the essential tips that you should take in launching an equity crowdfunding campaign:

Step 1: Prepare your company.
Remember that you'll be giving away marketing shares when you open an equity fund-raising campaign. To put it simply, you're selling company shares. For this, you have to ask a securities lawyer to create a shareholder contract. This contract contains the rights and responsibilities of shareholders. It also includes dispute resolution methods, shareholder responsibilities, share ownership, conflict of interest rules, asset management, business management, and share valuation.

Your lawyer should also help you create an offering document that you can use to sell shares to investors.

Step 2: You must set a funding goal.

How do you set a funding goal? Well, it's a matter of how much money you need for your business. But, that's not the only thing that you should consider in setting a funding goal. You should also consider your fundraising capacity. How much can you raise within the campaign period, say three months? Be realistic. Remember that only a few crowdfunding campaigns have managed to raise more than $100,000.

Step 3: Make your offering public.

Publish your equity offering on your website. It's also useful to post the offering on your official Facebook page, Twitter page, and Instagram account. As with any campaign, make use of all your social media outlets to spread the word about it. The wider your reach, the more interest you can generate for your campaign. You can also publish the offering in startup and investor forums. You can also ask help from your entrepreneur friends.

To get the attention of big ticket investors, it would be a good idea to hire a financial PR firm. These firms are well connected in the venture capital industry and can hook you up with a few investors.

Step 4: List your offering at a reputable crowdfunding site.

Now, you need to publish your offering on an equity crowdfunding site. It's wise to use reputable sites such as EquityNet and AngelList. You can also use Wefunder, Localstake, CrowdFunder, and Fundable. If you're running a real estate equity crowdfunding campaign, you should try GoFundMe and Kickstarter.

Step 5: Produce an equity crowdfunding pitch video.

Your pitch video must ultimately answer the question, "what's in it for me?". How would investors benefit from your company? Your pitch video must also contain the following company:

- ✓ What your company is about
- ✓ Why you need funds and what you're going to use the funds for
- ✓ Your product and its benefits
- ✓ Your company's market size and scalability
- ✓ ROI
- ✓ The current standing of your company
- ✓ The profitability of your company
- ✓ The projected growth of the company

Your video should be creative, but professional. You should also present yourself as an expert or a rising star in your industry.

Step 6: Ask help from your current shareholders.

Ask your current shareholders to participate in your campaign and help encourage potential investors. You can also ask help from your employees. Make it a team effort as everyone will benefit from it should the campaign be successful.

Step 7: Take time to verify each potential investor.

The JOBS act state that all investors in equity crowdfunding campaigns must be accredited. So, you have to take time to verify your potential investors and make sure that they are all accredited. But, what is an accredited investor? Well, an accredited investor is:

- ✓ An individual that has an income of over two hundred thousand dollars each year in the last two years. A married individual is considered as an accredited investor if he or she has a combined income of three hundred thousand with a spouse.
- ✓ An individual that has a net worth of more than one million dollars, excluding the value of the his or her primary home.

You can ask potential investors to provide certificates, securities filings, written confirmation from a registered broker or an investment banker, credit report, and disclosure of assets and liabilities.

Here's a list of documents or evidences that a potential investor can provide to prove that he or she is an accredited investor:

Type of Asset	Evidence
Real estate (not the primary residence)	Deed or title
Bank Accounts	Latest bank statement
Insurance	Latest statement
Securities	Formal valuation from a certified accountant
Cars and other automobiles	Vehicle title

All the evidence must not be older than three months. Also, check the registered owner of the asset. Is it under the potential investor's name or a company that he or she runs?

Step 8: Close the offering and file a form with the Securities Exchange Commission (SEC)

You should file a Form D (Notice of Exempt Offering of Securities) with the Securities Exchange Commission (SEC) within fifteen days after the first sale.

Step 9: Give your investors regular update.

Many entrepreneurs fail to update their investors. This creates doubts. To build a strong relationship with your investors, you must provide regular update. This show shows that you are one hundred percent committed to your business. This also shows that you are transparent and that you are not afraid to update and ask for feedback.

Step 10: If your crowdfunding campaign fails, try other funding options.

In case your equity crowdfunding campaign fails, examine your campaign and see where you went wrong. Also, don't be afraid to try other funding options.

Chapter 14

Crowdfunding Mistakes That You Should Avoid

Alright, so we have tackled everything that you MUST do in order to try and make your campaign as successful as possible. However, there are also things that you must avoid at all costs—think about it as learning from the mistakes of others. These things can easily cost you potential investors, even the credibility of your business and campaign. Keep the following in mind:

Mistake #1: Not having enough social media presence.
As discussed earlier in this book, social media presence is important in raising a lot of funds for your project. Sometimes, it's not enough to create a Twitter account for your project, you must also create a Facebook and perhaps an Instagram account. If you're not getting enough organic attention on Facebook, invest a few dollars in sponsored posts. This allows you to reach more people and generate more donations.

Mistake #2: Not telling your story.
Yes, you need to showcase the benefits of the product. But, you also need to tell your story. You have to outline the process of how you transform your idea into an actual product.

Mistake #3: Not creating high quality campaign materials.

Using low quality posters, videos, audios, and text can negatively affect the outcome of your campaign. It can ruin your credibility, too. So, you have to invest in high quality campaign materials. Avail the services of videographers, photographers, and graphic designers if you have to.

Mistake #4: Not doing enough research.

Before you start your campaign, you have to research and study similar campaigns. This allows you to adopt their best practices and avoid their mistakes.

Mistake #5: Not replying to inquiries and comments.

You have to engage your donors and make them feel important. Communication is key. Remember, these people are helping you out so and show them your gratitude by accommodating any questions they might have. Always allot ample time for interaction with both current and potential investors. This is all part of campaigning for your cause.

Mistake #6: Not having a marketing plan.

Remember that product development is only half of the work. If you do not have a robust marketing plan, you'll have a hard time generating revenue for your product.

Mistake #7: Setting an unrealistic goal.

Remember that a lot of crowdfunding platforms will not allow you to keep the raised funds if you do not meet the goal. If your goal is $100,000 and you only raised $10,000, the money goes back to the investors or donors. So, it's a good idea to set a realistic goal and budget. Never go beyond what you actually need as that could be suspect as well, and might even turn people off from investing in you.

Mistake #8: Not giving enticing rewards.

People will want something for the money they provide you with—nothing comes free anymore. It is important that you respect that, it is their hard-earned cash they're forking over, after all. Another good reason for offering enticing rewards is the fact that it also increases interest for your product. Think of it as your "bait". Get people interested, then hook them into the project through your passion towards the idea and how much you believe in it.

Mistake #9: Not doing the groundwork.

You have to start working on your project at least six months before you start your crowdfunding campaign. This provides you with enough room to work out any problems or unneccessary things that only distract from the true purpose of your project. The more streamlined and clearly defined things are, the better it will be for you and your investors.

Mistake #10: Foregoing proper budgeting and accounting.

This is important because people will be asking for receipts. Where is the money going? What are you going to use it for? Create a budget beforehand and account for every expense that you might incur during the process. This is important and would be very beneficial for you as well. If you have no clue where to begin, ask help from someone who has experience in the field or get the help of a professional. You will slowly learn more along the way!

Chapter 15

Crowdfunding Success Stories

In spite of the naysayers that have tried their best to criticize and discredit the viability of crowdfunding, there are actually a lot of success stories to tell. May their success be an inspiration for you to try crowdfunding and craft your own tale to tell others as well.

1. Oculus Rift

Are you a video gaming fan? Are you a fan of that popular anime Sword Art Online? A virtual reality head gear is a dream for some hardcore gamers. It's an idea that has captured the imagination of hundreds of gamers. And then VR head mounted display that is accessible to home gamers became a reality.

Oculus Rift was a huge success and it was celebrated when the first batch of VR gear were shipped in March of 2013. It was actually one of the biggest crowdfunding projects ever launched via Kickstarter. The fund goal to be raised was at $250,000, a modest amount come to think of it for such an ambitious project.

The actual funding that the founders were able to accumulate amounted to $2.4 million – well above their target. The gaming community and partners who had a vested interest in the success of the project were able to pull it through. According to stats provided by Kickstarter, they had 9 funding projects that were able to raise more than 1 million dollars in funds. The gaming industry is actually has several successful niches.

2. Shenmue III

This is an action adventure video-game. It's the third installment of the Shenmue series. The first installment was released in 1999, while the second installment was released in 2001. The video game director, Yu Suzuki, spearheaded the fund-raising campaign on Kickstarter in 2016. The campaign goal of two million dollars was reached in just eight hours. The campaign ended in July 2016 and has raised over six million dollars. The game will be released in December 2017.

3. The Pilot

The Pilot is first smart earpiece which allows for real-time translation between languages. In 2016, its creators launched a campaign to develop the project which garnered plenty of interest. It's one of the biggest success stories in crowdfunding, having raised two million dollars within a few months.

4. Kiva Microlending

Kiva is another success that reported a repayment rate of 98.93% -- no fraud there. Even though the concept behind Kiva is illegal in the US (loans are given directly to people and the loan amounts are provided by actual people), the company is able to carve their way to success.

The idea is to provide microfinance loans to people living in third world countries. They reach out to the poorest of the poor. They report that there are more than 1.2 million lenders in the US who participate in their fund raising. More than $550 million have been sent to the poor and destitute in countries outside of the US.

5. The Nikola Tesla Wardenclyfee Science Center

Nikola Tesla may not be as famous as Einstein or Edison, but he's a legend, an innovator, and an entrepreneur. The people behind the web comic called The Oatmeal are some of Tesla's biggest fan, so they launched a campaign in IndieGogo to preserve Tesla's old laboratory. The project earned one million dollars in just nine days. The Oatmeal used the money to turn the old laboratory into a science center and museum.

6. The Veronica Mars Movie

This is probably one of the most popular projects in the history of crowdfunding. Imagine filming a movie that is funded by the general public? Crazy isn't it? But the idea worked! The founders of the project were able to gather more than 5.7 million dollars.

7. The Coolest Cooler

Also known as the "portable party". The cooler comes with a phone charger, battery-powdered blender, cutting board, and a Bluetooth speaker. Ryan Grepper launched a fund-raising campaign on Kickstarter in 2014. The campaign goal is set at fifty thousand dollars, but they were able to raise thirteen million dollars.

8. SkyBell

There should be an app for everything, right? Well, what about an app that lets you answer the door and see who is ringing your bell? That's the idea behind the SkyBell app. It is pretty useful for people who work from home who don't want to waste their time walking to and from the door when someone knocks.

The app interacts with an audio and video system so you can interact with the people at your door from a distance by just using your smartphone or iPhone. Crowdfunding was used to fund this project. It's not the only one out there. Other app and technology projects have been quite successful.

9. FORM1

3D printing is the next level in the production industry. The only problem is that they are really expensive, home users just can't afford them. So the people behind the MIT Media Lab devised a way to create a 3D printer that is so affordable that the general public can get one in a jiffy. They funded the project via crowdfunding with an initial funding goal of

$100,000. By the close of their crowdfunding project, they were able to get 2,000 backers and a total capital of 3 million dollars.

These are only some of the hundreds of success stories in crowdfunding history. Note that not all successes require a million dollars. I have personally started a crowdfunding project for a small community charity. The goal was to reach $10,000 and we were able to hit that mark and exceed it by a few hundred dollars. Not much, but it was meaningful to the beneficiaries of the fund. On top of that, you could feel the community spirit as friends, neighbors, and other townsfolk pitched in to make the endeavor a success.

Conclusion

I hope that the information contained here was able to help you decide to get involved in crowdfunding. The next step is to contact a crowdfunding advisor to learn more about the setup process as well as how to build your funds when you have already launched your own campaign.

Here's a number of tips that you can use to launch a successful crowdsourcing campaign:

- ✓ Start working on your campaign at least six months before you launch the campaign. It's easier to lure people into investing in your project if you have already started some work on the project.
- ✓ Create a video to lure investors into investing in your cause.
- ✓ Do not try to win everybody over. You cannot convince a vegetarian to fund your beef farm. The key to crowdfunding success is to attract the right people.
- ✓ Offer an incentive to investors. This is the fastest way to get people to shell out money for your startup.
- ✓ Invest in your product design. Remember that aesthetic is everything, especially if you are trying to lure people to invest in your product and company.

- ✓ You have to incorporate crowdfunding into your schedule. You must engage your social media followers and post regular updates.
- ✓ Give your social media followers a peek on what's happening behind the scenes. This way, they'll know how passionate you are about the campaign.
- ✓ Do not make promises that you cannot keep. Before you're pitching an idea (not a product), make sure that you already have figured out a way on how to transform your vision into reality.
- ✓ Get your friends, colleagues, and family involved.
- ✓ Mail your rewards on time. Send an email to your donors in case you can't deliver the rewards on time.
- ✓ Do press releases. Also, reach out to bloggers and social media stars to help spread the word.
- ✓ If you have a budget, host a live event to increase the interest in your project.
- ✓ Use high quality text and photos for your campaign.
- ✓ The first few days of your campaign determine the success of your campaign. So, make sure to get your family member to shell out a few dollars for your crowdfunding campaign.

Remember that crowdfunding is like any investment opportunity. You can always start small and work your way up. It entails a certain level of risk, but the rewards are immense. Again, to your success!

By the same author

Available on CreateSpace